MW00803089

# Activist Mysticism: An Esoteric Teaching

Paul J. Goodberg

Helping Heal The Earth

*I am returned from pilgrimage,*
*I am.*
*I bring you blessings from Al-Andalus,*
*I am.*
*I bring you fire from Berat,*
*I am.*
*I bring you truth from Skopje,*
*I am.*

*You are!*

Activist Mysticism: An Esoteric Teaching

All rights reserved.

Copyright © 2014 by Paul J. Goodberg

For information address Helping Heal The Earth,
helpinghealtheearth.org or hhte@helpinghealtheearth.org

ISBN 978-0692208861

Published in the United States of America

Design and page lay out: Katja Gorup
Interior creation: David Tavčar
Project Supervision: Saša Petejan

# TABLE OF CONTENTS

# Introduction

In this moment, I am listening to a performance of Terry Riley's remarkable composition, "In C". I have paused to write this for you.

I am recalling a conversation some years ago with a young junkie. I told this man that for me the natural world is a church and God is hidden in the leaves, then the leaves become God. What does this mean? Simply put, this is an attempt to describe my experience of All That Is. Of course, there is no "I" in my experience. That which was the "I" has disappeared. Now the "I" is a convention.

This collection of talks that I gave between 2009 and 2013 is my meager attempt to verbalize my experience of what cannot be verbalized. My esoteric teachers taught me in complete silence, and I taught that way for many years. About ten years ago, I tired of the look of incomprehension on my students' faces, so I broke with tradition and began to experiment with words and sentences. Then I decided to stop being "hidden."

Hopefully, these collected talks sketch my development and outline some of my suggestions for the seeker of mystical experience. My emphasis is on experience rather than thought or belief. And while it is important for me to acknowledge my debt to both Western and non-Western teachers, I insist on the primacy of what is universal underneath the world's wisdom traditions. The universal opens to us in a leaf, in the sufferings and grief of our heart, and in the joys of sunrises and sunsets. The universal reveals itself after a lifetime of quiet and solitude.

As you read these talks, please remember to open to what is contained within the words and hidden between the lines. Perhaps in this way you, too, may experience that which is beyond words.

No introduction is complete without an expression of my gratitude to my primary teachers: Gussie Feldman, High Priest of Q'ero Don Manual Quispe, Lord Pakal of Palenque, and Sheik Ibn Arabi, the great Sufi saint, and to my academic teachers: Benjamin F. Nelson and Arthur J. Vidich, Graduate Faculty, New School for Social Research.

A second small volume of my talks will be published shortly followed by a third and fourth. We are preparing "Renewing the Esoteric Energy of the Earth: An Activist Teaching". The third volume is titled "Trauma and Esoteric Service" and the fourth is "Advanced Esoteric Service".

I send you my love.

Paul J. Goodberg
Corte Madera, California
October, 2013

# My Teaching

I'd like to talk with you about the path that I teach.

I don't offer any text. I have no text, I have no practices, and I have no belief system. I offer you no opportunity to have faith; rather, I invite you to develop your own experience of the sacred, your experience—not your belief, not your practices, and not your text—your experience of the sacred.

I also invite you to experience the sacred without expectation. Let it surprise you, because it is an It. It is outside of you, and It is inside of you. You are part of It, and It is part of you. You won't discover the sacred by exploring yourself, as Westerners are prone to do. All you will discover is your own self-absorption and how endless it can be.

To explore the sacred, to experience the sacred, for a Westerner, is an opportunity to become embodied. It is an opportunity to let go of concepts, thoughts, beliefs, and expectations and to allow yourself to be surprised. Because once you are embodied, you are, in fact, a larger intelligence than your mind and you have the opportunity to rediscover your essential nature. The more you are essentially what you are, the more capable you are of experiencing the sacred.

How do you get embodied? That is for you to discover. There is no universal answer for Westerners, like "If you do this practice or that practice, you'll become embodied." In fact, practice just keeps you stuck in your mind.

So how do you become embodied? You have to explore that. Why would you go through the process of becoming embodied? Why would you go through the process of rediscovering what you are essentially? Why go through the time-consuming, demanding process of learning how to experience the sacred? What could you hope to gain from it? What is the benefit? What would you get?

Well, eventually what you may get is freedom from personal suffering. The world may continue to suffer, but you get freedom from personal suffering. That doesn't mean that you stop feeling the pain of the world, but personal pain and suffering dissolves. And you get one other benefit, you get personal freedom. You get the capacity to live a life of choice. You become free of an extraordinary range of limitations. You don't have complete freedom because you are embodied, but the range of choices is extraordinary.

What do you not get? You don't get bliss. You don't get ecstatic, blissful joy. You only get the bliss state if you leave your body, and you are attached to your body by a slim thread.

The bliss state is an Eastern way. It is a passive state, a self–centered state, a state without empathy. It is a state that is withdrawn from the world. It represents an ideal state in the East, but as a Westerner, I am concerned about the state of the world. I am concerned about its pain and suffering. I am concerned about an ongoing capacity to be empathic, to care about the other, to experience what it is like to be in the other's shoes. I am concerned about service, about being an activist, about responding to the chaos and violence that we live in. I have no interest in being blissed out in some self-referenced state. I have no interest in withdrawing from service. If I am not embodied, I have no capacity to be empathic and others' suffering would be just a concept. If I am not embodied, I have no capacity to feel the pain and suffering of the world. If I am not embodied, I cannot recover the essential wisdom and intelligence of our species.

To begin, I invite you to take up the challenge to become fully embodied. Most of us in the West are afraid of it. We are afraid of our feelings, we are afraid of our emotions, we are afraid of death, we are just afraid. And, yes, the more you are embodied, the more fear you experience. So, paradoxically and oddly, to experience the sacred, you have to be willing to experience your own fear.

# My Background

Many times I have been asked about my spiritual background. I am going to attempt to sketch it for you.

Recently, my witness Sasa, who travels with me as I renew esoteric earth energies, said to me, "The reason you were selected to do this work is that you are neutral, you are affiliated with and partial to no spiritual tradition." I took that in and I repeat it because it is accurate. I could add, and I will add, that the one tomb that I would like to visit before I die is the tomb of Ibn Arabi in Damascus. That is important to me.

When I need inspiration, I read Ibn Arabi and other Sufi saints. I find them truly informative and inspiring. Recently I had an extraordinary dream. At the end there was a sheet of paper that read, "The only reality is The Real." If you don't know that type of talk, it refers to God, or Allah.

I have studied the Christians, I continue to study the Sufis, I read Buddhist writings, I read Hindu saints. All of it impacts me, all of it inspires me, all of it informs me, and all of it influences me. I respect all of it. I try to appreciate their strengths. I am aware of their weaknesses. (Each tradition obviously has strengths and weaknesses.) As Ibn Arabi famously said, "There are many paths to God."

When I was born, I was initiated into the esoteric lineage that had existed in my mother's family for centuries. It is central European. It is Polish. It is a lineage of healers and visionaries. My family never heard of the Kabbalah. I had never heard of the Kabbalah until I was a grownup.

The secret truth is that my family lineage is as much Gypsy as it is Jewish. In Central Europe, there was a huge mix of Jewish and Gypsy. It has never been written down. It is a mysticism and esoteric practice that is entirely oral. It is committed to service, and it is committed to devotion.

I don't teach that path. It is a family path. I don't practice that path. My family has no interest in that path, so I have no context for it. Perhaps my granddaughter, who is now a teen, will ask me to teach it to her. It is intended for her because it is a woman's path. We'll see what she decides. Meanwhile, that tradition exists inside of me and I would love to pass it along.

I intend to keep my neutrality. I intend to teach a spirituality that is as free of cultural baggage as I can make it. I intend to teach a spirituality that is not affiliated with any point of view. I am influenced by the teachings of Lord Pakal of Palenque. I am influenced by the teachings of Don Manuel Quispe of Q'ero. I am interested in and influenced by all of the saints whose graves and tombs I have visited and whose books and manuscripts I have read.

Please don't make the mistake of assuming that my teaching is committed to any tradition. I strive to be as free of the past as I possibly can. And I invite you into the freedom that you can experience when you step behind the veil.

# Basics of Mystical Awareness

## Daily Life as Ceremony

As we become grounded and celestially connected, we have the opportunity to reframe daily life. Our moment to moment experience can be ceremonial. Each moment becomes an intimate experience of the sacred. All moments are precious, all moments are valued. No moment is superficial or insignificant.

# The Process of Embodiment

When I was a young man, I was unhappy with the state, or the condition I should say, of my embodiment. I had a sense that I was nowhere near as embodied as I could be. And I knew intuitively that if I were willing to risk becoming more embodied, I would come up against all sorts of primal emotion that I found very frightening and ugly.

So being willing to become more embodied was in itself an act of courage. But I had no clue how to be more embodied. I tried all sorts of things. I tried fasting, I tried yoga, I tried mushrooms, I tried meditation. I can't even remember all the different processes and techniques I tried. Nothing seemed to work, and I was continually aware that I was afraid of becoming embodied. In fact, I became aware that I was afraid that I would die if I became embodied.

Finally, I decided that I would learn how to jog, which I did. I would jog for a couple of hours and then I would allow myself to slowly slip into a state of "no state," encouraged by the endorphins as well as my exhaustion and disorientation. I described it to a friend as meditative jogging or a meditative slow running. It was a state of simple, primal, awareness. It was a state of being embodied. I was finally in my body and the more I got in my body, the more I experienced anxiety, rage, terror, fear, hate, outrageous judgments. It just seemed endless, all the negative primal emotion that came up. It was as if I were puking.

I also became embarrassed, defensive, and self-rejecting—but I kept up jogging. I discovered that if I could get to the local high school track, a quarter-mile oval, I could teach myself to run with my eyes closed in this "no state." So I would jog around the track with my eyes closed, experiencing my body and all of its primal negativity. This, by the way, went on for years, perhaps a half-dozen years. Then one day I was done with it. I had puked up primal negativity all over myself. I had become intimate with myself. I had become embodied.

I tell you this for several reasons: First, you have to discover your own way to become embodied; there is no "the way" to become embodied. Then once you set out to become fully embodied, what you experience is awful. You experience all the primal crap that you carry around, that all of us carry around, and that we have stuffed down deep inside ourselves.

Finally, when you become embodied, you begin to connect to a deeper intelligence that has been buried inside of you and obscured all these years. You remember that you had been in touch with this deeper intelligence before you went to kindergarten. You discover that you can call it back because it is essential to what you are; and you can then discover that the life of the mind—your mind, my mind—is of great value when it is at the service of our deeper intelligence.

What I model when I talk with you is this marriage between a deep, inherent intelligence, intrinsic to what we are, and that of an active mind. I invite you to take the risk, become embodied, and discover what you truly are.

# Comments on Embodiment

If you are really embodied, you have the opportunity to truly experience what you are; and then in that condition, you are capable of experiencing the other, what the other is. That is an essential human quality. It is what we mean when we say that our species is a social species. To say that we are social, in the full sense, is to say that we are capable of actually experiencing what we are and what the other is. The whole issue in the history of this conversation is whether or not we also are capable of experiencing the other who is different from us, from a different group. As you know, this has been the rub in human history.

What has happened to us is that we are not in our bodies so we are alienated from our essential nature. If I talk about being alienated from our essential nature, it becomes conceptual. It becomes a rehash of 20th century concepts. If I talk about being embodied, I can be free of all the conceptual nonsense that has stifled this essential wisdom.

As I have said on other occasions, little kids are embodied; and now that I have a family dog, I discover that dogs are embodied.

# The Process of Grounding

There have been many occasions for me to discuss the process of grounding. Each of us needs to be grounded and to remain grounded. A simple way for you to ground is the following: Lie on the earth, on your back. Select a place that is not electric; select a place that is magnetic. How do we know? A magnetic place on the earth will welcome you and pull you down. An electric spot on the earth will push you up. It doesn't really want you. Electric places are usually places in urban and suburban areas, places of significant electromagnetic interference.

So, select a place that is magnetic and lie on your back. Relax, close your eyes, and breathe normally. Over time, you will come to feel the pulse of the earth, the so-called "Schuman Resonance," which is a measurable pulse. As you feel the pulse of the earth, allow yourself to open to it. It will, in fact, influence the pulses within your spine. Your spinal pulses, the fluids within your spine, will start to coordinate to the pulse of the earth. When you sense that coordination, you are truly grounded.

How long will it take you to experience this? Perhaps you will want to sleep overnight on the earth. Perhaps you will want to lie on the earth every day for an hour or so until you start to feel this pulse. Perhaps you will want to repeat this process indefinitely until you are actually coordinated with the earth pulse. That is what it means to be grounded.

# Grounding to the Earth

It seems to me that there is an important teaching here. What is it that I asked you to do? I asked you to connect, or ground, to the earth. And you are discovering that when you remember this primal relatedness, what you are changes, which speaks to how alienated you were.

I say this not to emphasize how alienated you were but to highlight a very simple necessity—we need to be earth connected, earth grounded. When you are fully earth grounded, the fluid in your spine is actually pulsed to the earth pulse. That is when you know the process is complete. Then you can just step out on the deck in the morning and there it is. You can feel it. Your whole being feels it. What you are is an animal, primarily, and you as an animal will feel your home in an intimate way. It is speaking to you. It is acknowledging you; and it is your responsibility to say, "Yes, this is my home, I do hear you. Thank you for receiving me. I'd like to be grateful to you. I am grateful to you. Thank you for this gift of keeping me healthy."

You can see one version or another of this all over the world, in places where people are living close to the earth. Walking with people who live close to the earth is a different experience of walking because they are walking on the earth as their home. It is a different orientation. And if you walk with them often enough, you will begin to notice something else: The person you are walking next to is conscious of her breathing. She is not just breathing, she is aware of her breathing. People who live close to the earth are aware of their breath. They are aware of the pulse, and they are aware of breath.

I invite you to remember the earth pulse and remember to be conscious of your breathing. That is a lot to ask but without our bodies being coordinated to the earth and without our breath being conscious, we are less than human. What is missing is our solidarity, our sense of commonality, our sense of being part of the aliveness of All That Is.

Once you become aware of your breathing, you will be shocked at what you start to notice, what you start to remember. You become aware that we are alive, each of us, and that everything around us is alive and breathing. We had forgotten this. Being alive had become just a concept. We had been less than human.

# The Celestial Connection

I am about to offer you a capacity. For some of you it is new, for some of you it is a repeat. It will allow you to be more effective or have an easier time with connecting celestially. This is not an invitation to merely open yourself to the heavens. I want you to connect yourself to a particular star or if you insist, a planet or a moon, but I would prefer a star. What you do is extend your field to touch that star so that there is an energetic connection between the star and you. You don't let go of your field. You keep your field and you extend it. You extend a thread, if you will, or a thin tube—however you want to hold that.

What do you extend it from? In principle, it should be the top of your head, but it is whatever it is for you. I don't think there is any necessity for it to be the top of your head. It can be anywhere that intuitively is correct for you.

The star's energy is invited to descend and come into the rest of your field. Once the energy has come into your field, let it go through your whole being. You can concentrate it in your hara if you feel comfortable with that. I would rather you not concentrate celestial energy in your heart center. Star energy is a general energy or a hara-centered energy.

If in the first few attempts you don't succeed, the stars will be out tomorrow night, too. This may take you several nights or you may get it on the first try. You may discover that you have always known how to do this because, actually, we do. It is part of our inherited capacity. So really, all I am trying to do is to help you remember. This is nothing new to our species.

# Remembering Our Humanity

I'd like to invite you to witness the earth by letting it pulse you, and I'd like to invite you to witness the stars by allowing one of the stars to enter you. We are earth connected and star connected, naturally, as a species.

When you allow the energy in your body to be primarily located below the waist, you are encouraging our memory of what we are as a species. When you become conscious of your breathing, again, you encourage our remembering of what we are as a species.

When you witness the earth and the stars, allow the energy to get out of your head and the upper part of your body, become conscious of your breathing, all of that allows for a very deep, strong remembering of who we are instinctively. We remember that we are compassionate, cooperative, affectionate and social.

And who we are instinctively is a species that attends to the material from a location within the non-material. That is our natural way. I am looking for you to remember what we are naturally. What our species inheritance actually is.

# Life Behind the Veil

When I was about 50 or so, I arrived one afternoon in a very remote region of the Andes, the Q'eros region. I got there before it had become a stop on the spiritual tourism itinerary, it was still largely untouched. It was traditional Andean village life. These were llama herders and potato farmers. And seasonally they would go down into the jungles to grow other crops. There were less than a thousand of these individuals at the time in just a few villages, and I was the only European in the region. I was a guest and I felt quite at home, quite comfortable.

I met adults who could not read or write, who had never read a book, who had no passport, driver's license, or credit card. They didn't know how to use a toilet, didn't use a knife and fork, and didn't know what day of the week or even what year it was. It was an odd experience for me.

What I discovered quickly was that certainly the adults and the teens and the older children could all, if they were comfortable with you, tell you how you looked. Not your clothes, but what we call your energetic field. Everyone looked at me as energy. That was a routine skill that everyone had.

They also played instruments, they weaved, they looked after llamas, they could farm, they could do all sorts of things, and they could tell what I was because they could read what I was. They could talk about it, but to them it was like breathing, so unless I asked, they wouldn't talk about it. The impression I made was an energetic impression.

24

Their day-to-day, hour-to-hour, moment-to-moment life was that of being present. They knew no other way; they were completely present, completely embodied. What they said and what they did was obviously sourced from a very deep intelligence that is our common inheritance. They were remarkably skillful and adept at the life they lived. They were inventive, creative, and smart. But, their intelligence was not mental, it was not conceptual, it was not from intellect. In fact, they had very little intellectual development. They also had very little of what we call personality, and they didn't have a lot of opinions.

Within families, there was love and affection, there was kindness; yet I experienced, which seemed really odd to me, their struggle to be empathic with me. Because most of them had never met a European, they didn't like my smell, it was offensive. They had no body odors.

They had never seen the kind of clothing I had on, nor had they seen processed food. I had endless supplies of energy bars, and within a week my entire supply was gone. The kids from all the villages came by to eat them. They had never tasted anything like it. They thought it was a great treat, so I gave away my energy bars and was stuck eating potato soup and llama meat.

They couldn't understand anything about me. It was very hard for them to be empathic, to get into my shoes. It was really confounding to them and, of course, it was very hard for me to get into their shoes. It was quite an extraordinary experience for all of us. I liked them immediately and, surprisingly, most of them liked me. They were confounded and confused about how to be empathic with me, but they never stopped trying.

What I noticed about them was that all of life was an ongoing experience of reverence—all of life was reverence structured ceremonially. I had read about that in endless ethnographies, but I had never experienced it. And there it was, it was true. The ordinariness of their reverence was to me extraordinary. Every moment was an opportunity for the ceremonial unfolding of reverence. All of life was experienced reverently.

At one point, I had a startling knowing that these Andeans didn't live in material reality. They looked after their llamas, they looked after their needs, they took care of whatever needed to be taken care of materially;

but they didn't live in material reality, they lived in non-material reality. Their typical day, in all of its ordinariness, took place behind the veil. They lived in a mystical awareness.

The shock of that was actually too much for me for a while. None of the ethnographies had ever talked about any of this. These remote people, herders and farmers, lived behind the veil. They lived in sacred space, sacred time. To them, it was completely ordinary, and you wouldn't notice it if you were stuck in the material yourself.

Needless to say, I felt extraordinarily at home there, and it was my only direct personal experience of being in a social setting where the mystical was lived as the ordinary.

# Basics of Activist Mysticism

## Foundational Values

The seeker may value humility, reverence, kindness or service. Without foundational values the seeker becomes lost in selfishness and self-obsession.

# The Witness

I have talked about the witness for two or three years. Today, I want to talk about the witness from the point of view of how I personally experience witnessing at this time in my life.

When I listen, when I deeply listen to what wants to be known, what seeks to be known, what wants to make itself known, that is my witness. Witnessing is being attentive, is listening, actively listening to what wants to be known, what is seeking to find me.

As I conducted the healing earlier today, I was listening to what wanted to show itself to me. I was listening to what was seeking me. I was witnessing what presented itself to me. I did not create what was to be known, I didn't cause it. It wasn't an interaction between me and what wanted to be known, I simply witnessed it. I paid very close attention; and little by little, what wanted to be known as I witnessed it became known and I could conduct the various steps in the healing.

As I teach and as I heal whatever I am asked to heal and proceed in the ways I am asked to proceed, there is no difference to me, at this point, between an act of listening and a very careful witness—they are one and the same.

# The Witness: An Update

One of the topics that I've attempted to verbalize is that of the witness. I have discovered recently that the witness is more or less a buzzword. I didn't know that, and I am sorry to say that I have discovered it is being used in ways that have turned it into a cliché.

I first encountered the term "witness" when I was a teenager. I joined Quaker demonstrations against nuclear testing in the atmosphere. We understood ourselves to be witnesses, witnesses for sanity. I continued to work with that sense of being a witness, a witness for social justice, a witness for human rights.

At some point in my own service, I decided that I needed a witness. As I have said at other occasions, my first effort at healing a battlefield when I was a teenager was a dismal failure. I really was overwhelmed by the darkness at Gettysburg battlefield in Pennsylvania. I was alone, and I continued offering land healings until a time in my early 60s when I decided to stop offering these healings alone and to ask for a witness. I wanted a social context. I wanted there to be a consciousness, in addition to mine, that was present for these healings.

Over the last ten years or so, I've had a number of witnesses, sometimes one, sometimes a group, and they have provided a social context. I've continued to wonder what else was embedded in my experience of having a witness. I began to understand that a witness offered both a social affirmation and, more important, an empathic connection. For me to be witnessed is to experience another, the other, who is capable of empathically affirming, supporting, connecting to what I am doing. Without the empathic connection, the act of witnessing is incomplete.

What do I mean by "empathic connection"? How can I be witnessed by the other? As I ask about the empathic connection, I have come to understand that embedded in witnessing is respect, trust, and the capacity to get into my shoes. To be properly witnessed, what I experience is being trusted, respected, and understood.

I have come to see that this is an essential quality that each of us must bring to our communication with the other. Can we respect the other? Trust the other? Get into the other's shoes? Then we can support the other, communicate with the other, and share social reality with the other. When this type of witnessing is present, we have genuine relatedness.

# Listening, Witnessing, and Mirroring

As I've said on a number of these occasions, from my point of view, I am teaching what I call an active form of mysticism. It is a mysticism that focuses on service. And within my description, I've talked a great deal about listening, about listening to what wants to be known. I want to remind you that it is not meditation, it is not contemplation, it is listening.

Meditation for most of you is a prelude to transcendence, and I insist that we stay embodied. Contemplation, as it is used in the West, maintains duality. Listening, as it has been practiced traditionally here in the Americas, is an insistence that there is information that wants to find me, or that may want to find me, or that doesn't want to find me. Nevertheless, there is information that wants to be known, however paradoxically it emerges.

There have been years when nothing has been known to me: I haven't heard anything. There have been years when what I have heard is contradictory and confusing. And, gratefully, over the years, certainly in my 60s, I have had the consistent blessing of clear information that wants to be known as long as I am patient enough to wait for it.

It is never convenient, it is never on schedule, and it shows up when it shows up. Sometimes it is brought to me by the wind. Sometimes it is brought to me by ocean waves, by the sound of streams. Sometimes I hear it inside what a child is saying to me. Sometimes a bird speaks to me; it is inside the bird song. Sometimes I hear what I am listening for very early in the morning, when there is a very fine silence.

I usually don't like what I hear. It is consistently inconvenient, challenging, and unpleasant. Sometimes it is so unpleasant that I keep listening in hopes that I will hear something else. Sometimes I'll ask, "My God, please, this is not really for me!" and I'll wait around in hopes that I'll get some kind of a modification.

Whatever it is, I will say yes to it, which is why I am teaching this weekend. I would have preferred not to teach this weekend because I am still tired from my last trip to the Balkans, but my information was that it was time to teach a weekend before the weather turned ugly. It is also time to conduct the ceremony that I am conducting and that I am asking you to witness tomorrow.

So what does it mean for me to witness a ceremony? I've been a witness. I was my last embodied teacher's witness. I was Don Manuel's witness. What does that mean? Why was I Don Manuel's witness? There were plenty of students, earnest students, and I was his only witness.

To witness is to be an embodied mirror. To truly witness is to mirror back what you witness.

I spoke at great length about this at my Palenque teaching this past February and talked about witnessing Lord Pakal. I have talked to you about witnessing Limantour beach. In order for you to be effective in the esoteric, not to contemplate it, not to meditate in it but to actually interact in it—to actually have an impact on it and then to have an impact on the material plane—is to learn how to mirror whether you mirror a bird, the wind, Limantour beach or me.

Your goal is to learn how to mirror so that you can truly witness, so that you can actually become activist within a mystical awareness, within a mystical context. How do you do this? You must let go of your story, I mean radically let go of your story. And it is true that I really don't care to talk about my story. I don't care about my story or your story. It is not of any interest to me. I mean that radically.

As you let go of story, you let go of the artifice that maintains it. Then you can let go of your story about your story. (I have noticed that those students of mine who have made some progress in letting go of their story

34

have a story about letting go of their story.) I don't mean that to be unkind, I just want you to see what that is.

So, letting go of story is the key to witnessing. The witness is the mirror. Over time you may become a clear mirror.

It was alleged that Ibn Arabi was God's perfect mirror.

# Deeper Listening

As you listen and watch what I am offering, ask yourself how you pay attention. What are you paying attention to? Are you focused on my words? Are you analyzing what I am presenting? Are you categorizing it? Do you have reactions to it? Judgments? Approvals? Or are you attempting to listen and see what is in between the words, what is underneath the words?

I am inviting you to experience what I am offering in the spirit in which it is offered. This isn't a teaching for your intellect. This is a teaching for your being, all of you; and if you can listen with your body, if you can listen with your deeper awareness or deeper intelligence, then you can connect to the way I am speaking. You can absorb the energies I am offering that are in between and underneath the words. If you just take in the words, it is actually not that interesting.

The way I am teaching represents and exemplifies what I am teaching. It is your challenge to stop listening with your intellect and open yourself to a deeper listening.

# Are You a Spiritual Junky?

We can distinguish between levels of development and experiential states. It is possible to have a range of experience that has no impact on your development. It is possible to have extraordinary openings, revelations, exhilarations, ecstasies, epiphanies of all sorts that in a week or two are just memories. A large number of people go from teacher to teacher seeking out these highs, these exhilarations. These are the spiritual junkies who can't get enough highs. This is not development. It is junkie behavior.

Why? Because the experience is a mental, a mind experience. It has no larger significance. It doesn't have an impact on what you are. It doesn't matter how many drugs you have taken, you are still the same. It doesn't matter how many spiritual highs you have had, you are still the same.

How you experience is more important than what you experience: How you experience as a body, as the fullness of what you are.

If your spiritual experiences do not allow you to become more reverent, then you are not developing. And if you are not becoming more empathic, you are not developing. You are simply getting high, then it wears off and you are back to being who you are: unhappy, looking for a healing, looking for new capacities, and restless.

I invite you to allow yourself a full experience, an experience that actually takes place outside of cognition, that can't be explained and maybe not even understood. Yet, mysteriously, that sort of experience will help you to become more empathic and more reverent.

# Living a Sacred Life

Much of what we understand as esoteric practice is actually natural to us. It is only that we have forgotten. We, in the West, have become so mind oriented that over the centuries we have forgotten our own natural intelligence. Our deeper intelligence has been lost to us, and what we think of as our instinct is often just fight or flight. The rest of it has been lost to us. My intention is to help you revive deep memory; and once you start to remember, you will be surprised at the actual capacity you have to live in the non-material. It is our natural way.

Yes, it is more difficult now, in the 21st century, to cope with the material when you reside in the non-material. There is the ever-present danger of being over-stimulated and when you reside in the non-material, being over-stimulated is actually quite painful. So you have to develop skill sets that allow you to cope with the ever-present potential of being over-stimulated. Each of us has that particular challenge. There is no guide book that will help you to cope with over-stimulation.

In fact, the popularity of the teachers from the East who are monastic and ascetic is an odd popularity in this regard. They have retainers, they have staff, they have helpers, and they don't cope with over-stimulation. They have others do that. You and I, we have to cope with the danger of over-stimulation and the pain of it. It is our challenge. It is a new challenge. It is a very difficult challenge.

We also have to cope with a story that is offered to us, the one that says we need endless practice. Practice is only necessary to revive your memory, your deeper memory of what you are. Once you remember, you don't need any practice. Continuing to practice at that point will start to bring back a state of being mindful, of being in your mind that will make living in the non-material very challenging if not impossible. I invite you to step out of mind, to live in the sacred, and to conduct yourself from the deeper intelligence that is our inheritance, which is not mind based.

I continue to use my intellect for all sorts of specifics but I speak to you from a place inside my being that is not my mind. I speak to you from my deeper intelligence, which is my birthright as a member of our species.

# Student Development

It has been my experience over the 25 years that I have been teaching, both in the United States and in Europe, that those who attend my teachings, whether they are weekend or weeklong teachings or those who have gone on my healing journeys, tell me how much they have changed, how much they have been benefitted, how significant the experience is—and then two weeks later, four weeks later, I discover that they are unchanged, that they are who they were prior to attending the teaching or the healing journey. In fact, for the most part, students have a dim memory of what happened.

One of the motivations for these transcribed teachings is to remind those who attend my teachings what was said because there is a tendency to literally forget, or as I have come to refer to it, to have amnesia. There have been very few exceptions, less than a handful in 25 years.

In general, those who attend my teachings have no long-term benefit. They are essentially who and what they were before we met. How can that be? If you listen to my teachings without experiencing what I am offering, if this is some version of a TED talk where you get excited, it is interesting, and then your entertainment is over and you are on to the next consumption, then these teachings are just another mode of spiritual entertainment.

If you don't experience the teachings, they have no significance. If you take these teachings in with your mind, you are wasting your time. These teachings are not for your mind. If you insist on returning to your regular life after hearing my teachings, if you do not allow these teachings to have an impact, if you don't allow yourself to grow because that is disruptive to your current life, then you are just involved in another form of consumption.

I have had numbers of my students say to me, "After I have spent time with your teachings, I go through the process of re-entry." "I resume my ordinary day. After all, I have a lot of important work to do; I have responsibilities and obligations, and so forth. So thank you and I will check in with you next time."

Another version of this is, "Well, thanks, I feel better; but now that I am back to my ordinary life, I feel the way I usually feel." Or, "Thanks, I have a new capacity, I can do something special, I am special. Thanks for helping me with my self-esteem (or my ambition)."

What was different about my own point of view as a student with my teachers? Fundamentally, I had a relationship with each of my teachers, a relationship based on reciprocity and empathy, a relationship of trust, affection, mutuality, and genuine experience of the other. This relationship existed throughout the time that I remained a student with each of these teachers, and throughout my life I have maintained this relationship in memory. Without this high quality of relatedness, I could not have been these teachers' student; they would have dismissed me.

So the positive opposite of being a consumer is to actually take the risk of having a genuine relationship with me. Why is it a risk? Because you come up against your own fear: your fear of intimacy, your fear of exploitation, your fear of being inadequate, your fear of failure, your fear. It is very risky.

It isn't possible to develop spiritually without a substantial relationship with a teacher. You can have an exalted experience, you can have an extraordinary high, but it is just another junky experience. Without a real relationship with a real teacher, you don't develop.

# Living Behind the Veil: Part 1

In my experience of teaching, I have witnessed many students who have stepped behind the veil, during a retreat or a healing journey, or during an extended one-on-one time with me. For the most part, after our contact is over, most students do not stay behind the veil. They re-enter their ordinary material life and let go of their non-material life behind the veil.

When I ask students "What happened? Why are you no longer where you were?" I don't get a clear answer. What I am usually told is, "I need to be effective. I have a lot of e-mail, a lot of meetings, a lot of shopping ... a lot of whatever." As if it isn't possible to live behind the veil and attend to the material life.

When I suggest that it is possible to live behind the veil, to reside in sacred space and still attend to material life, what I mean to say is, "Really, why did you go back to living in the material world? Why did you let go of your sacred space?" Or to put it differently, if you are to continue to live in the non-material, in the sacred space behind the veil, that is possible only if you have a significant ongoing relationship with a teacher. Without that relationship, you will not be able to stay behind the veil. If you are not witnessed by a teacher and, reciprocally, if you do not witness the teacher, if that relationship of mutual witnessing is not maintained, you will inevitably return to where you were. This has been my experience over 25 years.

It is also my experience that if you have an ongoing viable relationship with a teacher and choose to live behind the veil, you will experience an absence of personal suffering; although you will continue to experience the suffering of others you will experience an extraordinary freedom, an extraordinary range of choices. As you live your life behind the veil, within the sacredness of All That Is, what you will discover is that the life you live is not a static life; it is a dynamic, evolving life. You continue to develop, you continue to grow, and you will continue to grow until you let go of this body. Life behind the veil is not a static state.

My experience and the experience of my principal teachers is that the sacred space is an evolving, ongoing space that you inhabit as a participant. The sacred space grows and you grow, and the sacred space will continue to grow indefinitely. As I said, you will grow until you let go of your body.

So I invite you into a relationship of mutual witnessing with a teacher who is capable of assisting you in your development.

# Living Behind the Veil: Part 2

In my experience as a teacher and as a student, and in my experience with students when they step behind the veil, I see there is a tremendous emotion of grief that comes into everyone. I remember my own grief because I thought it would kill me. I thought I would literally suffocate in my own grief; and it wasn't grief for me personally, it was grief for suffering that had nothing to do with me. Also, when I witnessed students who had either personal grief or grief for the condition of the planet, or both at the same time, the grief that comes up is so strong that it is hard to feel safe. It is hard not to get terrorized by this extraordinary grief.

This is unavoidable. This is what happens because grief is stronger than love. Pardon my being "incorrect," but grief is stronger than love. Love does not dissolve grief. Nothing dissolves grief. Grief will stay as long as it stays and after a while, you become skilled at grieving. You actually become skilled, there is a skill set that allows you to grieve and go on with your day.

When I started to learn the skills of grieving, it shocked me because I had experienced grief as immobilizing. But little by little, I was able to continue to grieve and go on with my day. Now, at this point in my development, I have an ongoing experience of grief for what I witness, especially as I travel, and that is only one of my experiences in the day. It is not THE experience. Or, to put it differently, it is part of my experience of my day.

When I look back on the first half dozen years of my adult life behind the veil, I see it was marked by intense grief. Yours may not be as prolonged. Mine was, and it led to my becoming very skilled with grief.

It is also my experience that living behind the veil isn't safe. It is not that I feel endangered; I feel threatened by the constant possibility of being over-stimulated. It is in that sense that I don't feel safe. When I come to a retreat center like Ratna Ling, I feel safe here because I don't get over-stimulated. There is no stimulation other than the fox that walks by, or my time spent with all of you, or sitting looking at the trees, or going for a walk or whatever. I don't feel threatened by being over-stimulated.

My two principal teachers lived in a world where there was no over-stimulation. They never had to confront this issue. This was a non-issue for them. It is a non-issue for those who live behind the veil and are essentially ascetic or monastic. However, for those of us who live in this world but are not of it, it is a real issue. And the issue gets stronger as there is more and more stimulation, as each of us gets more e-mails every day and there is more available information, and more of whatever. There is always more of something that is demanding our attention. We do get threatened. The danger is that we become distracted. If we get really distracted, we can lose our grounding, our celestial connection, we can lose our embodiment. We can start to get lost and confused.

I acknowledge that here is a great challenge for us and that the wisdom of living behind the veil was developed at a time when there was no over-stimulation. For us, it is very different.

# Living Behind the Veil: Part 3

Life behind the veil has significant challenges. When you have arrived behind the veil, you are confronted by an enormous experience of grief that can go on for months or years—your grief, personal grief—and you are also confronted with your experience of the pain and suffering of the world, which is another type of grief, as you know.

If you find yourself alone, without relationship, living in the non-material, living in the sacred, living behind the veil, you run the risk of becoming paranoid or monomaniacal or narcissistic. If you are not in relationship, if you are separate or isolated, all sorts of intense emotional reactivity is possible and, in fact, is likely. Historically, we have seen this over and over again. If you are behind the veil and you are not in empathic relationship with at least one other, all of these unfortunate psychological consequences will occur. It is very likely.

At another level, there is a very important issue that has to do with your values. If you have penetrated the veil and you are living behind the veil, my wish for you is that you have strong values so that your behavior is not exploitive, it is not self-serving, and it is not self-indulgent.

One of the responsibilities of your teacher is to make sure you have strong values: values of respect and values of integrity. Without strong values, you will turn quite decadent and sink into the abyss.

# Human Perfectibility

Check and see that you are here, that all of you is here and present. See that you are grounded. See that you are not caught in your thoughts. See that you are not too busy to pay attention in a deeper way. Check and see if the way you are listening to me will really allow you to absorb what I have to offer or whether it will just stay as thoughts and concepts. Check and see if you are listening with your body—that all of you is listening.

In some way, what I am attempting to do is to help you to step out of a Western mode, into a more mystical mode that is native to the Americas; that originates in the Americas, and that has resonance with what is ancient in Europe. It is almost impossible to find it in Europe, and it is becoming increasingly difficult to find in the Americas. But I am not offering archeology, I am offering a way of being that is traditional and supported by the land here in the Americas.

Much of what I have been saying during the last ten years is, I suspect, unintelligible unless you are experimenting with it as a way of life. Listening to what wants to be known is an ongoing practice, not listening to thoughts or feelings but listening to what wants to be known. That is foundational. What wants to be known is more important than thoughts or feelings. What wants to be known isn't personal. It doesn't carry a personal preoccupation. It is the deeper layer of all existence. It is not Truth, it just is what is.

I am aware of the responsibility of speaking in a way that is useful and helpful, of speaking about what wants to be known. I am aware of what

I would like to speak about, and that is not what wants to be known. What I'd like to speak about is what happened in Poland. What I'd like to speak about is the volcanic ash, but what wants to be known, what I have been told over and over again to talk about, is the topic of human perfectibility—a topic I have never talked about.

I have said that I have given up being hopeful and despairing. They both seem like a trap. The underpinnings of being hopeful and despairing have to do with the belief in human perfectibility. I gave that up, too. There is no such belief in the Americas. And in the tradition I was raised in from Central Europe, there is no such belief: there is an insistence on love and kindness, an insistence on being aware of all the connectedness, an insistence on the sacred nature of life.

As long as we are in a body, we can never be perfect. The older you get, the more your body ages and the more obvious that will become to you. The older you get, the more unreliable your body becomes, the more unpredictable it is, the more problematic. So whatever degree of development I have at any one moment, whatever my level of awareness is, I am always reminded of the distractions of my body. My body is always a distraction. Perhaps I will become perfect when I leave my body. We'll see (laughs).

The awareness I cultivate is not about leaving the body while I am still alive, it is not about transcendence; it is about being willing to confront both hope and despair as a trap.

I spent many years experiencing my anger, rage, and grief. I did not deny them. The Westerners I know who skip over their anger, rage, and grief are haunted by these emotions even though they pretend that they have transcended them, or put them aside. But we do have the opportunity to fully experience our anger, rage, and grief and to heal these very powerful emotions. And as we heal these emotions, our heart can be cleansed and then we are truly capable of loving.

So our challenge is to be able to love. If we believe that we can become perfect, we miss the opportunity to love and we become trapped in hope and despair. If I insisted on perfectibility, I don't know how I could respond to volcanic ash and the potential health hazards that may follow from it.

48

I simply acknowledge that the earth is alive and will survive. With its survival, living beings will survive. I will continue to do the best I can in spite of all the damage by offering healings to the earth. Do I have hope about my healings? Or despair about my healings? Or hope that ultimately the earth or any of us will become perfect? No. Rather than being distracted by a belief in perfectibility, I am doing what I can do and I continue to invite each of you to listen to what you are told to do.

Without serving the earth, without serving all living beings, we are inevitably caught up in selfishness. The only way that you can avoid the selfishness that the spiritual path generates is by service.

# Activist Mysticism

## Soul

What are we?
We are soul in a physical container.
What is soul?
Soul is God's mirror.
How do we mirror God?
We rediscover our natural empathy.
What is spirituality?
A polished mirror!

# Activist Mysticism

This is not a teaching for the mind. I am not teaching content, I am not teaching concept—I am addressing this teaching to your being, to your deeper knowing. Please drop down into a deeper level of awareness so that you are receiving what I am saying not filtered through the mind. If you don't know how to do that, just have the intention to listen without the mind. That is an intention; it is listening without the watcher, that which watches and keeps asking "Am I understanding this? Am I getting it?" It is the watcher who is getting in the way of listening directly. Instead, take what I am saying into the body and remember that the energy I am transmitting is more important than the words. The energy is really what I would like you to take in, only secondarily the words.

The teaching I would like to offer is a so-called postmodern teaching. It is a teaching in what I occasionally have called "activist mysticism," or an activism grounded in mysticism, an activism grounded in a direct communion with spirit. This activism, unlike contemplative modes, is meant to have an impact both on the subtle planes and on the material plane. This activism is what Europeans in the 18th, 19th and 20th centuries termed shamanic. In the 21st century, it is a mysticism that is activist.

The term "shamanic" has taken on so much baggage, especially with the development of spiritual tourism and all of the nonsense that flowed from Castañeda and his imitators, that the word itself is just a buzzword. But really the word was meant to describe a mysticism that was observed by Europeans in Siberia, in Tibet, in Central Asia, and in the New World. It is a body-based mysticism. It is not transcendence, it is an embodiment.

The embodiment is only possible if you are completely connected to the natural world.

What does it mean to be connected to the natural world? You are connected to the divine essence that is the natural world. You, an embodied being, connect to the divine essence of the natural world. And who is the "you"? You are a living soul, an embodied soul. So you, an embodied soul, connect to an embodied divine essence called the earth. Then you never let go of that connection. That connection is 24/7—not only during a meditation. That is who you are, or who you become if you are not that way now.

As you allow yourself to connect to the natural world, you, an embodied soul, listen. You patiently listen for what you hear. You listen to the wind, you listen to the birds. You listen to the deeper resonance of the earth, the so-called "Schumann resonance," the vibration of the earth, because the earth has its own measurable and unique vibration. You listen. You practice patient listening. You don't ask questions. You don't look for answers. You don't get into some alert mode for omens or signs. You simply listen patiently. What are you listening for? You are listening for that which wants to find you. You wait for what is looking for you. You'll only know what is looking for you if you are listening. If you are distracted, if you are not fully embodied, you won't notice what is looking for you.

There is very deep information that will come to you. Not on your schedule, not on material time; it will come to you on divine time. You might listen for days, weeks, or months before you hear anything. In divine time, that is just the blink of an eye. You practice patient listening and as you commune as an embodied soul with the divine essence of the earth—the earth's soul if you will—as you listen to what wants to find you, you will notice that naturally (because this is natural to our species) there is another connection that occurs. You will find yourself communing with the stars. It is likely that you will find yourself establishing an affinity, or even a communion, with a particular star. That is certainly how it has been historically in the Americas. Those people who lived here before their way of life was disrupted were communing with the divine essence of the earth and the divine essence of a particular star. So the embodied soul that you are deeply listens, connected to the earth's divine essence and the divine essence of a star.

At my birth I was connected to a particular star. That connection was established by my first teacher. If you have difficulty connecting to a star or believe that it is more appropriate for me to gift you with a particular star, let's talk about that one to one. That is a traditional ceremonial process in Central Europe, Eastern Europe, and the Americas. I don't know about Asia and Africa; I have no information about that.

What I am offering is a structured awareness connected to the earth, connected to a star. The process is deep listening, or active listening. I am not suggesting you become involved with channeling, spirit guides, and angels, devas or anything of the sort. Please, don't go off into some imaginal flight of fancy. Listen deeply, and inside your being you will sense information for yourself. Your soul will know what is legitimate. Your soul doesn't want angels or spirit guides. Your soul wants a direct connection. The upper world will directly communicate to you when you listen. It may speak through a bird, it may speak through the wind, it may speak through the earth's resonance, or it may speak through a twinkle of a star. It will speak directly to you. It is not mediated by any of these imaginal concepts (angels, spirit guides, etc.). Please.

When someone tells you that they are channeling, whatever that means, that is not what I am describing. The information I get is very clearly direct communication. It is not in words, it is a much deeper sense but I do know what it means. You will know what it means as you learn how to listen and learn how to understand. We are talking about creating mystical knowing, or knowingness, based on being fully present within a larger awareness.

There are practices of activism that can be termed shamanic. Some of those might interest you, some of them may not. But the foundation for whatever practices interest you or don't interest you is this deep awareness, this fully embodied, deeply connected, patiently listening awareness.

# Reciprocity

In February, 2010, I found myself at Palenque, in Southeastern Mexico, talking about topics and information that I had never expected to talk about, let alone have recorded. Most of you have a copy of that. I am going to go over some of that material and extend it and try to put it in more simple terms. Again, I am trying to verbalize what wants to be known, not necessarily what I am comfortable talking about or even would otherwise be willing to talk about.

I remember being in my 20s, some 45 years ago, sitting in my first cultural anthropology class in graduate school. The professor, Stanley Diamond, and his teaching partner, poet Jerome Rothenberg, were talking about this topic I knew nothing about, called shamanism. I was listening to them talking about what was called primitive people of the third world and their systems of magic.

As I was listening to this, over the weeks that I listened, I became more and more confused because what they were describing was me—except I had never been outside the United States. In fact, I had not been much outside of New York. I had been trained in New York, yet I could do almost everything they were talking about, easily. I hadn't realized that I was "primitive," or that I had come from the "Third World," or that I was somehow "tribal."

So I came to understand that what was meant by shamanism is what I now see as a type of active mysticism. I was trained in traditions from Central Europe that were oral traditions, exclusively oral. These are not

Kabbalistic traditions. There has been an attempt to co-opt my teaching into a Kabbalistic system, but it is not Kabbalistic, it is oral; it existed for who knows how long. I know that within my lineage there is Gypsy influence and there is Yiddish influence and I don't know what else. When I was initiated as head of my lineage, there was no lineage tree that was passed on to me, so I just don't know. And the objects that I was given at the moment of my initiation as the head of my lineage are typical magic objects, ordinary household objects that are endowed with special significance, just as you would find in a so-called primitive tribe.

There came a time when I wanted more training. Well, there is nowhere to go in Europe. Everybody who actively practiced mystical systems is dead. There is nowhere to go for training. I have looked—trust me, I have looked. I don't mean I have looked through my meditations and through my travels, esoterically; I have gone and looked physically. I went and looked in every place that I had dreamed of that there might be survivors of these traditions. There is no one.

That is why I went into Latin America. That was the next place to look for additional training in the activist modes of mysticism. I am not a contemplative. I wasn't trained to sit around and meditate in some remote place, or to sit around and pray in some remote place. I was trained to help through active service. That is my point of view. I was not trained to spend my life quietly in seclusion. The lineages that existed and that my lineage is part of were all active, they were service oriented, and I find that I do my best teaching in the context of service. That is why, when I get together with you for a day, I like to go out and offer healings so we are not just sitting around not helping, not being of service. I find that selfish.

What I am teaching is ultimately a Central European-based mysticism that is highly active, that is informed by my additional training among indigenous people. It remains an active mysticism. People say to me "Well, are you a shaman?" I actually hear that as racist because built into that term is a devaluation of native forms of mysticism as somehow inferior to Western or Eastern forms of mysticism. I am a practitioner of an amalgam of different types of mysticism.

My focus is to offer healings. For me to offer a healing to the earth is to recognize that the earth has consciousness. If the earth had no consciousness, it would be dead. It has consciousness. All living plants, animals, birds, trees, all of it have consciousness. It is within that knowing that I offer a healing. When I offer a healing to an individual, it is within the awareness that that individual has consciousness.

The land and individuals do not have an infinite capacity to receive a healing. The ability of a land or an individual to receive a healing has to do with the extent of the openness of the land or individual that I am offering a healing to. If the land is damaged, it is not very open, it can't receive much. If an individual is damaged, she is not very open, she can't receive much. Then there are all sorts of dynamics having to do with the back and forth of my offering a healing, and that dynamic back and forth is what I mean by reciprocity. We are in relationship with all living things and if that relationship is not reciprocal, we are exploitive.

To be aware, is to be aware of our relationship with all of consciousness. To be in relationship, we can't be taking. If our relationships are not based on kindness, on some sense of service, on some sense of respect, we are just taking.

Respect is the reciprocity, the relatedness. As we offer consciousness, consciousness is offered to us. Often we have to initiate. Because so many people and so much of the natural world are damaged, often we have to initiate, we have to offer something: some kind of service, some kind of respect. It will be returned if you are conscious enough or awake enough to notice. The more you offer, the more you notice that the world mirrors back to you what you offer. And the way I have been describing how I actually work is to say that I initiate the relationship. There is an acknowledgement, reciprocity, a mirroring back, and then I offer a stronger energy that has a higher vibration that will get mirrored back. Then I offer an even stronger energy that has a higher vibration, and so forth. That is the process of offering a healing. That is how it actually works.

That process is difficult if what you are offering is to something or someone who is damaged. You may have to offer a great deal before anything is mirrored back. In fact, the first time you offer something, perhaps nothing is mirrored back. Perhaps tomorrow it will begin to be mirrored back to you, or the next day. It depends on your generosity.

What I am saying at another level is that within the emerging spiritual community in the United States and in Europe, as this postmodern spirituality develops, there is no particular interest in service. There is an interest in self-development but no interest in service. What we are seeing is an extraordinary selfishness, an extraordinary self-absorption, and a rather ferocious narcissism. Without a spirit of service, there is no glue to the emerging spiritual community. We tend to fracture and fragment, and we tend to get isolated from the rest of consciousness as we focus on ourselves. What separates me from almost everyone I teach is that I am not focused on myself. Almost everyone I teach is entirely and exclusively focused on themselves, regardless of their rhetoric of service.

I am acutely aware of this phenomenon having lived here in the heart of the spiritual community in the United States over the last 25 years. I am living in a community characterized by intense self-absorption, selfishness, and excessive narcissism. Many of the individuals living here are highly developed spiritually; but there is no real community cohesion or spirit of community because there is no sense of service. There is no sense of being concerned about anyone else except as they can help you. My response to that is "Well, how much service are you doing? What are you actually doing? How are you participating in the larger consciousness? Are you offering love? Are you offering kindness? What are you doing? Or are you taking care of yourself? And do you see that as either/or?"

In all of the traditions that I am trained in, there is no selfishness. There is no narcissism. Self-development is largely unknown. Why is self-development important to us? We come from families that are damaged, so-called dysfunctional families, so we have to attend to our emotional issues. None of my teachers came from damaged families. They didn't have emotional issues. Well, we do, so we have to attend to them. If we don't, we never get very far. We are always reactive and unstable. So, yes, you have to attend to your emotional issues. If you don't, if you think that by developing your spiritual awareness that allows you out of your emotional issues, you are making a terrible mistake. And I continue to teach many people who have not resolved their emotional issues, who are basically unhappy and depressed and angry and moody.

So, we have to be attending our emotional issues because our family backgrounds are dysfunctional. We have to attend to them so we can put them aside and go on with our development. We have to come to the understanding that what we are is manifested awareness, what the planet is, is manifested awareness or consciousness. What we are is manifested consciousness, which is what we are. We have a possibility of actually cultivating our awareness, our consciousness, so that we come to understand how we are connected with All That Is, not as a principle but as an experience. If you don't experience your connectedness, you really can't offer service, it is just a concept.

# Living in Reciprocity

We are just back from offering healings at the Presidio in San Francisco, Crissy Field, Fort Baker in Sausalito, and the Golden Gate itself from Fort Baker. And this morning we were at a Mayan calendar ceremony in San Francisco's Golden Gate Park, led by a Mayan Elder named Don Pasquale. It is the Day of Human Perfection, so we went to that ceremony. It is the end of the Mayan ritual calendar and the beginning of the new Mayan ritual calendar.

From my point of view, all of daily life is approached as the experience of the sacred. All activity, all responsibilities, all tasks, all communication, every moment of the day is an experience of the sacred; it is an expression of the sacred; it is a life lived within the context of the sacred.

All of life can have a ceremonial or ritual character. Academic anthropology has commented for over a century on this quality of indigenous life in remote villages. My experience has shown me that it also is possible to live that way here in the First World, in a metropolitan area. For me the only exception to that is when I am driving a vehicle. I have never been able to drive a vehicle as an expression of God, as a communion with God, as an experience of God. But other than driving a vehicle, I am reasonably clear that the rest of my day is lived within a ceremonial or ritual context.

What that means, of course, is that I am not focused on multitasking, I am not focused on productivity, I am not focused on getting things done, I am not focused on being effective or efficient. My focus is a devotion to doing God's service, to being in the service of God; and within that focus, each moment has meaning and significance. There is always an opportunity to be of service, to express God.

The relationships that I have with those that I encounter are reciprocal relationships. There is mutuality, reciprocity, a give and take, a relatedness that acknowledges my obligation and the obligation of the other to be in relationship to each other. My relationship to people, to things, to the natural world, is a reciprocal one. And here in the First World, I have to work at that because very few people agree with me. So the reciprocity is more from my point of view than it is from those I am interacting with. Within the natural world and the world of things, there can be a reciprocity that is much easier to achieve than it is with other people.

Reciprocity is a bedrock operating assumption of indigenous cultures all over the Americas. It has different formulations in different cultures, but it comes down to the basic sense of relatedness or reciprocity. And, of course, when Europeans came to the New World, indigenous people presumed they could be related to mutually, reciprocally. By the time indigenous people realized that wasn't the way the Europeans were, it was too late. The Europeans had taken whatever they wanted. It wasn't that the indigenous people were naïve. It wasn't that they weren't smart. It was simply that their worldview was not about taking, it was not about dominating, it was not about selfishness—it was about sharing within a point of view that what we are sharing all belongs to God, that everything is God.

For me to share within the point of view that everything is God means that I live ceremonially with the intention of being reciprocal; and because everything to me is God, as it has been historically in the Americas, the experience of God involves both the experience of the physical energy of All That Is—the energy of people, birds, rocks, the natural world—and the experience of the subtle energies, the hidden energies, that require a mystical orientation, an esoteric orientation to apprehend.

What got labeled by Europeans as shamans or medicine men or curanderos, or whatever they were labeled as, is simply the New World's mysticism, the trained capacity of a minority of individuals to apprehend and be in reciprocity with the subtle energies, the more refined energies of the sacred.

I find myself increasingly uncomfortable with the term "shamanism" because it has a kind of baggage that doesn't allow us to apprehend that really it is an active mode of mystical experience, of mystical awareness, of mystical expression, and it is a mode that is indigenous to the New World. It is not a mode of contemplation; it is a mode of relationship, of active relationship within a reciprocal point of view. So my relationship to the subtle energies is reciprocal, it is active, there is a sharing, there is a mutuality. I find the contemplative modes foreign and uninteresting. The activist modes call to me, specifically the activist modes of healing, restoration, and renewal of the planet.

# Healing Journeys

I'd like to start this talk by speaking about two very interesting books. The first is a book by the Armenian esoteric, Gurdjieff; the second is by the Sufi Master, Ibn Arabi, who originated in Andalusia. Both of these books are instructive for us.

Gurdjieff sets out on a journey to discover hidden esoteric truth: teaching that is held by obscure and remote teachers in obscure and remote places. Ibn Arabi sets out to find the saints buried in the tombs of cemeteries, and he spends his youth visiting these tombs. He receives teaching and energetic transmission.

What I make of all of this is very important for me. As a student, I wanted additional teaching; I wanted access to wisdom traditions. I was willing to go and find them, and I travelled all over the Americas and over much of Europe, listening, sitting, walking, driving, being with tombs, being with teachers.

Sometimes these are referred to as pilgrimages, sometimes journeys. I use both words interchangeably. These are my ways of receiving additional teaching, visiting sacred places that have energetic transmissions, visiting wisdom teachers willing to share with a seeker. For me, these journeys are a necessary supplement, an expansion and a deepening of my training. As I approach my 70th birthday, I have to tell you that I still receive energetic transmissions. They are still of great value to me. I continue to present myself for instruction, for information, for added capacity.

I have also in the last 25 years taken students of mine on these journeys: I have taught my students how to receive what is offered. The skills of the seeker are difficult skills to learn because we have forgotten how to listen, and we have forgotten how to seek. We have, unfortunately, become tourists.

These journeys are particularly important for us because all over the world the esoteric teachings, the esoteric teachers, and the tombs and sacred places have been under assault for centuries. The sacred sites are hidden. Teachers are mostly dead. Traditions are hard to find or have been forgotten. We go in search of what is near extinction. Nevertheless, we can receive a substantial education in the esoteric if we are diligent and sincere, if we learn how to listen, learn how to seek.

# What I Am Learning about Healing the Earth

Today I'd like to start by telling you the state of what I know. It is a cliché that your teachers leave it up to you to figure out what they haven't taught you. Every teacher does that. They offer you some of what they can offer and you have to figure out the rest. Or they offer you what they know and they give you transmissions to capacitate you, and you have to live the capacity. So I am living the capacity.

When I travelled to Central Europe, to Poland and the Czech Republic, I took on the challenge of releasing all of the souls that were wandering around, who had been traumatized and couldn't find their way home, who were lost and confused and inadvertently creating a lot of negativity. I released as many souls as I could in Poland and the Czech Republic, focusing on zones of high incidents of death: concentration camps, cities, battlefields. I also made an effort to revive the land, the natural world, in these zones I focused on; and to one degree or another, I think we had some good success in Poland and the Czech Republic.

Before this, and before I embarked on the two trips I made to the former Yugoslavia, I stopped in Padua, Italy. I found the energetic remains of a saint, from a 6th century church, and I revived her and asked if she would spread her love throughout the old medieval walled quarter of Padua. I released wandering souls, cleared land, and cleared buildings. When you go to Padua, now, you can feel this female saint.

Then I went to the old City of Verona, near Padua (both are in Northern Italy), and I found the patron saint of Verona, an African woman. I revived her and asked her if she would once again radiate through the old quarter of Verona, and Verona is quite different now.

Later I traveled to the former Yugoslavia, a place where civil war is still very fresh because the warfare had gone on in the 1990s. You know, civil war is a very particular kind of passion. Neighbors kill neighbors. It has a particular quality to it; it is remarkable. People who know each other are killing each other. That is the nature of a civil war.

The International War Crimes court for the former Yugoslavia took a really radical step and decided that rape is now a war crime for the first time in International law. As you may know from history, rape was used on a massive scale in the civil war in the former Yugoslavia. It was an instrument of war, as it has been historically in Europe and all over the world. Here it was acknowledged as a war crime, and there were people who were tried and convicted of the war crime of rape. It was brand new. It was also the first time a criminal court convened for a civil war and that court is still functioning. That war ended in 1999, so it is recent, although the main fighting was in the early '90s.

By now I have travelled through most of the former Yugoslavia. What I discovered was that there were three energetic centers in the former Yugoslavia: Belgrade, Sarajevo, and Ljubljana. I revitalized these centers, reconnected these regions to their centers and cleared the land of its grief and negativity. I released wandering souls and healed the tear in the energetic grid above the earth.

Then I asked for the same gift that I asked for in Trieste when I healed that city. I asked that in each of these centers the divine feminine be gifted to the energetic center of each center so that the divine feminine, the Eros, the creativity, could once again be manifested throughout these three regions. Each time I asked, the divine feminine appeared, and the way these regions now feel to me is that they are actually healing. There is actually the re-emergence of Eros, creativity, love, healing. Finally, I connected each of the three centers, so there is a larger unity again, at least energetically. I am continuing to learn and discover how to go about healing a city, a region, a country, and it is really no different than when you go about healing a person. So that is a summary of what I have learned and what I have been able to help achieve.

Will everything I am doing result in a shift in the collective? On the first trip, I tried to address the collective, the negativity in the collective, in the same way that I might try to address the negativity in a person, by trying to directly dissolve the negativity. It just didn't work. The way to address it, it now seems to me, is to re-establish energetic coherence and energetic bonding so that the collective has an energetic coherence, and then to offer the gift of the divine feminine. That is how I am now addressing negativity in the collective. I am looking to re-establish a collectivity that is not disintegrated, that is re-bonded, and that has a healing quality.

The re-establishment of energetic centers and the threads I have sent out from the centers to these regions re-thread all the areas of the region to the center. I am recreating the structure that once existed before the civil war. I had to re-create the structure of community, or bondedness, introduce the divine feminine into the structure, and then allow that to work, which is what is going on. Without the gift of the divine feminine, I don't think what we are after in terms of true healing would really be occurring.

But the deeper energetic center of the former Yugoslavia is Sarajevo. It is actually the heart of it. I am not able to revive Sarajevo because its culture is destroyed. Culture is about people. When the people are killed, or flee for their lives, the culture is destroyed.

# Nathan of Gaza

I am going to talk about a topic that is very difficult to verbalize for me.

Perhaps you know or have heard of a man called Nathan of Gaza. He died in 1680 in Macedonia. After his death, his grave was a pilgrimage site until it was destroyed sometime in the 1940s or 1960s, it is not clear when.

I was recently in Macedonia looking for his grave. I am convinced the grave really is destroyed. His writings are not available. They are held in an archive that is not open. There has been a concerted attempt to erase his memory.

A few years ago, I stood outside the Vatican at the spot where Nathan of Gaza stood. He stood for a week in that spot intent upon healing the darkness of the Roman church. He had travelled a great distance, many miles, to arrive at the Vatican to offer this healing but Nathan's healing was incomplete.

In the hour or so that I stood there, I completed the healing that Nathan had begun. The Roman church is now simply decadent but no longer actively dark. It has been an honor to complete Nathan's work in Rome, and I am sorry that I could not find his grave. I wanted to pay my respects to an extraordinary healer and visionary, whose life embodied the principle of active mysticism, or activist mysticism. He was an esoteric master committed to offering kindness and healing to the material world.

# Nathan, Sabbatai, and the Challenge of Empathy: Part 1

I want to speak to an issue that has been in my face. When we were in Berat, Albania, I had the startling experience of discovering the tomb of Sabbatai Zevi (I have a picture on my desk). So what is important about Sabbatai Zevi and Nathan of Gaza to me? Well, for one thing, Nathan really is someone who set out to confront darkness in the material world and was extraordinary in his devotion and capacity to confront that darkness. Very few highly accomplished mystics ever took on a task like that.

At another level, what is important about Sabbatai Zevi and Nathan of Gaza is that these highly developed esoteric masters both turned megalomaniacal. They were so effective, so potent, so extraordinary in their capacity and impact that they became highly distorted by the results of what they did.

So for me, they are a huge caution.

# Nathan, Sabbatai, and
# the Challenge of Empathy: Part 2

Empathy is what anyone who is offering healings must have and maintain in order not to become distorted, so I have a very intense concern about maintaining my capacity to be empathic. And as my young son approaches his teen years and gets more and more outrageous, I am constantly challenged.

I have the example of my two principal teachers who remained empathic; and as I said, I have the warnings of what happened to Sabbatai Zevi and Nathan of Gaza. Additionally, as you probably know, there is a long list of highly accomplished spiritual teachers and healers who have gone off the deep end and turned out to be an embarrassment.

So, yes, I am engaged in a service project, which Sasa Petejan witnesses and you support, that is helping to heal our planet. It is something we are doing as our service. That is all it is.

## About the Author

At 72, Paul J. Goodberg speaks softly about his direct experience of what is "hidden." He lives in Northern California with his Parisian wife, the former Patricia Aouate, their teenage son, Teo, and four year old rescue dog, Babba.

Made in the USA
Thornton, CO
09/26/24 04:47:03

a836d2e1-b259-429d-8571-35b7b84c2c3aR01